Your message is one that will resonate with many. Enjoy life, love the ones that share your life and there is more to life than work. Unfortunately, many of us don't realize these lessons until faced with a health scare much later in life when most of it has passed us by. You have put these life lessons front and center and challenged the reader to act. You've also given the reader the opportunity for change, the beneficial reasons to do so and left it in their hands to decide their own fate. The first half of the book tells the reader why it was important for you to change and hopefully allows them to see some of themselves in your story and the second half demonstrates the implementation of change. After reading your book I realized that I need to exert more control over my life instead of my life being in the hands of another. Have a plan for life so that life doesn't plan you.

Kevin Corcoran, Esq.
Vice President and General Counsel
BOB SCHMITT HOMES, INC.

First of all, don't let the title fool you. Even though a dentist writes it, the message is applicable for anyone that's ever owned a business or been in a management position. Killing the Practice Before It Kills You is a poignant synopsis of how all the seemingly little things, and our reaction to them, are what truly shape our lives. If you feel like your life is out of control, and your business is running you rather than the other way around, this book is a must-read.

Patrick A. Thompson, D.D.S.
Joplin Dental Care

Dr. Ron's book is an antidote to dentists, hygienists, and teams that operate in a mediocre haze. Thanks to your insights I think and react differently to the things that happen in my life and my office. Thirty-five years ago, I would have laughed you out of the room and told you to go to hell! I am a better person because of you. I have a daily vision for myself that makes me the best that I can be. I cannot tell you how that mantra gets me through a rough day.

Shawn Petrillo Molchan, RDH
Registered Dental Hygienist

As a chiropractor I am all too familiar with the term "burnout." You feel like a gerbil running on a wheel with no purpose or direction. Dr. Arndt's wonderful book gave me hope. It helped me realize that I am not alone in my frustration. By applying just a few of the concepts contained in his book I felt empowered with a new focus to take control of my life and get off that wheel. I have already made positive changes in my practice to bring balance back in my life. I now enjoy going to work again.

Phillip E. Barry, D.C., C.C.S.P
Chiropractor

Every dentist faces a multitude of challenges in their practice and life. Ron Arndt, as both coach and dentist, provides great insight into the delicate balance of work, family, and self. You'll discover a template for life changes, and in some cases, truly save your own life. A must read. I couldn't put the book down!

Charles Blair, DDS
Author, Coding with Confidence, inventor of PracticeBooster™, and dentistry's foremost authority on practice profitability, analysis, and overhead control

The message was frightfully clear to me. As a type A personality myself your book jolted me to realize that I must "shift" my ways and learn how to have fun again. Just like the cliché, this book is as "serious as a heart attack!" Dr. Ron's insights have been a huge wake up call for me. Life isn't all work and no play. You encouraged me to realize that change begins with me. You proved the point that, "it's never too late to shift your thinking!" Change you did! Thank you for this gift.

Mr. Tom Lamoda
District Sales Manager, GC America Inc.

Spot on!! Dr. Ron's book should be required reading for all newly licensed health care professionals, not just dentists. Get control of your practice from the get-go; not twenty years later. Some things are more important than weekends and nights at the office. Read his book to discover the value of planning your personal and professional life well—you only get them once.

Charles Norris, OD
Optometrist

A SELF-CARE SOLUTION FOR DENTISTS AND
OTHER HEALTH CARE PROFESSIONALS,
BUSINESS OWNERS, AND MANAGERS

Killing the Practice
Before It Kills You

HOW THROWING OUT MY
BUSINESS MODEL SAVED MY LIFE

By **Ronald F. Arndt,** DDS, MBA, MAGD
THE DENTAL COACH©

Library of Congress Cataloging-in-Publication Data

Arndt, Ronald F.
  Killing the practice before it kills you : how throwing out my business model saved my life / by Ronald F. Arndt.
    p. cm.
  ISBN 978-0-9816822-7-3
  1. Decision making. 2. Leadership—Moral and ethical aspects. 3. Success in business. I. Title.
  HD30.23.A76 2011
  658.4'062—dc22
                                          2010022640

Text © 2010 by Ronald F. Arndt

All rights reserved. This book may not be reproduced in whole or in part, by electronic or any other means that exist or may yet be developed, without the permission of the author.

Editor: Tricia Brown
Designer: Aimee Genter

Arnica Publishing, Inc.
2880 SE Eight Ave., Suite 110
Portland, Oregon 97202
Phone (503) 225-9900; Fax (503) 225-9901
www.arnicacreative.com

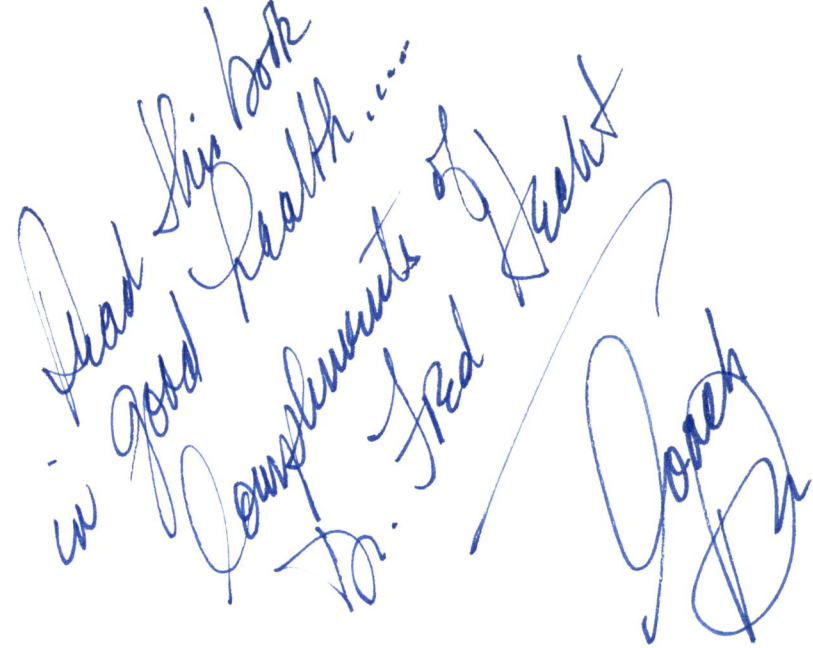

Dedicated to "Sweetness" (my wife, Trish) and to my "favorite oldest daughter," Ashley, and my "favorite youngest daughter," Brianne, my three most prized life treasures.

TABLE OF CONTENTS

xi	Acknowledgments	
xiii	Introduction	*The Seat-of-the-Pants Approach*
1	Chapter 1	*First, Stop What You're Doing*
9	Chapter 2	*How'd I Get Here Anyway?*
15	Chapter 3	*Life Does Not Happen in a Vacuum*
21	Chapter 4	*Gerbil Wheel Dynamics— He Can't Run Forever*
27	Chapter 5	*What's Most Important?*
35	Chapter 6	*The Workplace Makeover*
45	Chapter 7	*Killing the Practice*
65	Chapter 8	*The Business of Business*
77	Chapter 9	*My Heart Attack Gift*
95	Chapter 10	*Finishing Well*
101	Resources	

ACKNOWLEDGMENTS

Silent gratitude isn't worth much to anyone. And because I believe that "No one is as smart as all of us," I must thank Trish Arndt, my wife, whom I have nicknamed "Sweetness," for the genesis of this book. Years ago, after I published my memoirs as a personal gift to my two daughters and, ultimately, their children, Trish was persistent that I write this book. She recognized that there is a story in each one of us and insisted that I share a part of mine. I believe she did this with the hope that others may benefit from all my mistakes. Trish is my daily celebration. Remember in *As Good As It Gets*, when Jack Nicholson says to Helen Hunt, "When I'm with you, I want to be a better man?" That's what Trish does for me.

My daughters, Ashley Hammond and Brianne Arndt, have truly been my best teachers. They kept me from developing the horrible disease *psychosclerosis*—the hardening of the attitudes—and for that I am grateful. They taught me that we don't see things as they are, we see them as we are. They taught me how to be a better dad, because our children become what we pay attention to. I'm proud of them, as they are magnificent young women.

I want to acknowledge my brother, Dr. Scott Arndt, for being at my side, and for his guidance and patience with me through this entire process. That also goes for Lisa Filka, EFDA, my incredible Expanded Function Dental Auxiliary. If I could "steal" her away from my brother to work in my coaching practice, I would do so.

A very special acknowledgment goes to Mr. and Mrs. Mike Melnyk for their immeasurable support and for making me feel like the son they never had.

What a wonderful gift to have been introduced by my friend, Brock Dumont, CFP, to a patient and understanding publisher, Ross Hawkins, and he in turn paired me with editors Tricia Brown and Kathy Howard. Without these lovely human beings, my message would never have been coherent. Through their gentle encouragement, I learned that what I thought and felt, I created, and I have created what I believe. I hope you will enjoy it.

INTRODUCTION

The Seat-of-the-Pants Approach

HAVE YOU EVER BEEN ASSIGNED A TASK, taken a new position, or tackled a project with essentially no direction or instruction? Think about the outcome. Did you make lots of mistakes? Were you embarrassed about struggling? Did you wonder what others were thinking? Did you tackle the project aimlessly, using the seat-of-the-pants approach? I've been there, too.

The startling truth about dental school: there was little or no training on practice management techniques, business training, how or where to set up a practice, how to hire, or how to market my new business. I didn't know what a profit-and-loss statement looked like, let alone what to do with it. At graduation, I was awarded my Doctor of Dental Surgery

(DDS) degree, a slap on the back, and the phrase, "Go get 'em, Tiger!" I was thinking, *Now what?*

Throughout my dental training, there was no direction or support for the big decisions ahead. No mentor programs existed for students. Sometime in my junior year of dental school, important questions started to swirl in my head, such as:

Should I join the service?

Should I work as an employee?

Should I become an associate or partner?

Should I consider a General Practice Residency or specialty training?

If I set up my own practice, how do I find the right location?

What kind of practice do I want?

Where am I going to get the money to begin?

Where do I go to get help and what questions do I need to be asking?

Equally overwhelming unknowns were related to the nuts and bolts of running the business itself, such as: How do I hire people? What's the process, the pay, the position descriptions? How do I talk to a banker? What are the steps to negotiating a lease? The list went on and on. They never told us how to

Introduction

set up and operate a profitable practice. According to the late Walter Hailey, cofounder of an organization once known as Planned Marketing, the ability to establish solid business systems, caring patient interactions, and business savvy contributed to 85 percent of a dental practice's success.

If you're a dentist, I suspect you can relate to these fears and challenges. If you're in a different field or profession, I imagine the same questions nagged as you were trying to launch your own business.

As dental students, business and practice management instruction was absent from our training. Oh, there were one or two classes that were labeled "practice management," but they were of little value and had no connection to the real world. We were coming out of dental school thinking we knew so much. The dental training was exhaustive and demanding, yet from a business perspective, I was an "unconscious incompetent" and didn't know it.

I entered my professional life wondering how I would be able to pay back my school loans, start a practice, purchase equipment, and have money left over to repair my beater car. Like a sightless person in a strange city, I set out. My management style could best be termed "seat of my pants."

My learn-as-you-go efforts to establish and grow my practice nearly cost me my life. Over the course of the next two decades I stumbled forward thinking each step must be the right one. I believed working harder was the logical, time-tested solution to resolving heavy school debt, personnel problems, and personal deficits. In spite of my business ignorance, my practice was growing, but so was my overhead. I became so obsessed with running the business that I insisted on earning an MBA. At a young age, I accepted that the best way to predict my future was to envision it and then live it as if it were real.

I was active in the community with Kiwanis, the Chamber of Commerce, school levy committees, and pancake breakfasts. You name it, I got involved. I was taking in excess of 125 hours in dental continuing education every year. I pampered my team, lavished them with benefits, took them on junkets to the Bahamas, St. Thomas, and other high-powered practice motivation programs . . . all under the misguided hope they would perform better, stay with me longer, and help me grow my business. I wanted them to like me, too. Meanwhile I was simultaneously attempting to get my business under control without really knowing where I was going. What was my destination? I was the gerbil running on the wheel . . . never catching up, always on the run, no time to stop and catch my breath. Going, going, going.

Can you relate to this situation? Some might say it's because I'm a type A personality. But what I've found is whether you're a type A or type B, the only solution is identifying a need for change and acting on it. As for me, I didn't have the tools or the sense to get off that gerbil wheel, discover what I wanted, and formulate a plan. Up until this time, I had failed to take the time to declare what was most precious and important to me.

Looking back, I'm certain that my childhood set the stage for me to develop this convoluted belief system, and yet I was determined to not blame my dysfunctional youth. Even with a good marriage and two great kids, I felt so alone in the midst of all this activity. I was stressed and directionless, and in need of someone to help me find my way. I had no balance in my life.

It shouldn't have come as a surprise to me, but it did. At age forty-one, I suffered and survived a heart attack that would have killed me had it not been for the helicopter transport to the Cleveland Clinic. In the span of a heartbeat, I discovered what was most important: staying alive for the benefit of my family. As I lay in the emergency room in excruciating pain, I thought: *What has my life amounted to? What am I going to do? How did I get here? How do I get out of here?*

My wife Trish stood close to my bed while the ER team was frantically working on me. "Are you okay?" she asked. "Why are you crying?"

"It's not right for the kids to grow up without a dad," I answered.

Instinctively, I saw the heart attack as a gift from God. It was the wake-up call that I so desperately needed, forcing me to revisit where I was going and how I was living my life.

In the weeks and months that followed, I made a personal commitment—more than that, I was on a mission—to define which aspects of my life I wanted to keep and develop, and which ones I should discard. No more would my wife be a single parent, lacking my presence, putting up with my inattentiveness to her and the kids. No more would I try to please everyone. No more would "work, work, work" be my mantra.

I began to change everything. That sounds so easy or cliché, doesn't it? But when your life is on the line, the picture becomes clearer, and so does the urgency to make big changes quickly.

Introduction

I knew about the dual theories on making change. Some say to tackle the low-hanging fruit, the easy things first, that gaining momentum will make the other shifts easier to take. Then there are those who aspire to *massive* change, and fast! I chose the latter. The incidence of a recurring heart attack or worsening health after the first one is rather high. According to a 2008 American Heart Association study, for a person age thirty-five or older, the odds of a recurrent heart attack within a year are 1 in 492.6. The chances of dying from a second heart attack are significantly higher than dying from the first. Recurrent heart attacks account for 14 to 30 percent of all hospitalizations for heart attacks, but they are responsible for 30 to 50 percent of deaths caused by heart attacks.

I did not have the luxury of taking my time. The details of what I did with my home life and my practice, the life lessons I learned, are what I want to share with you.

How do you know if your business is killing you? Take a moment right now and consider this checklist. Have you ever experienced any of these warning signs? Check off those that reverberate with you.

- [ ] You find it difficult to get a good night's sleep because you are thinking or worrying about the business.
- [ ] Your attention is on home when you are at work and on work when you are at home.
- [ ] You tell your spouse they are number one in your life when silently you are more focused on the success of your business. After all, it's who you are!
- [ ] You act happy and content on the outside. In reality, your insides are churning and you never feel in control.
- [ ] Your energy level begins to fade, and you make excuses when you know you have not been taking care of yourself. You pass it off as something else.
- [ ] You are too busy to play those "goofy" games with your kids, who are so hungry for your attention.
- [ ] You read the newspaper or business journals when your spouse is talking to you because you have so much to catch up on. Then you fall asleep after twenty minutes, because you needed "just a little nap."
- [ ] On a weeklong vacation, it takes three to four

days to unwind. You feel like a new person for one or two days, then the tension builds again, welling up uncontrollably, tightening every muscle. Sunday nights are the worst.
- ☐ If you want something done right, you have to do it yourself. Only you can do it, because it takes too much time to explain and delegate a task to another person.
- ☐ You hear this voice in your head: "I don't need anyone else. I'm smart and can do it all on my own."

If you checked off a single one consider this a "red flag." Don't pass it off as inconsequential. The accumulation of these signs slowly and insidiously over time can be deadly.

I've written this book in the hope that you will not repeat my mistakes. If you have even the slightest hint that your business is draining your life energy, perhaps even killing you, then this book has been written just for you. Take action and discover the sweetness that life has to offer. Get off the gerbil wheel and create balance that works for you. I'll show you how.

CHAPTER 1

First, Stop What You're Doing

HOW DOES A GERBIL GET OFF THE WHEEL? He stops what he is doing.

Work-related stress is epidemic in America. A 2004 survey by the American Psychological Association tells us that two-thirds of Americans say they are likely to seek help for stress and 54 percent of Americans are concerned about the level of stress in their everyday lives.

It was a constant for me, too. I was growing a large practice, producing in the top 5 percent of dental practices nationally, and creating a reputation for being a strong dental businessman. I was always working, doing everything I could to grow the practice. My argument was, "Hey, I have to keep working like a mule. I have to do whatever it takes to protect and support my family. What that means is work more, work harder, work, work, work."

When you hear all the gurus describing the ease of bringing in another doctor, the cost savings involved with sharing expenses, and the wonderful camaraderie that results when two or more doctors come together, oftentimes they gloss over the realities. They may fail to tell you about the additional stress of making certain that the practice can support the other doctors; stresses from the additional business management issues; stresses over communication between not only the doctors, but between the different staffs from the two practices; and in my case, three practices. Additionally, there is a massive emotional drain that is rarely if ever discussed. This can become costly to your health and psyche.

As a young dental practitioner, I found that the best, easiest, and the most fun way to grow the practice was through positive and personal relationships with my patients. I also discovered something about myself that's common to many of us dentists. We fall into the trap of thinking that there is a direct relationship between how much our patients love us and how much we talk to them.

We have such a need to feel valued, appreciated, and even loved by our patients that we think that if we talk unendingly and make them feel like we're best friends, that they, in turn, will value and appreciate us even more. I'm convinced this incessant talking is a coping mechanism for a lack of confidence.

Ultimately, after this entire monologue, the hope is that patients will request we perform more dentistry on them or their family. So, I found myself spending excessive amounts of time talking with my patients, thinking they would love me more. What I failed to realize was that falling behind in my schedule was also adding to my stress. Plus, I grossly overlooked the fact that patients are not really interested in small talk. Rather, they wanted to get in and get out of that dental chair as quickly as possible. Now don't misunderstand, of course they want a warm connection with their dentists. They want to feel special and cared for, but they have time commitments and busy lives that demand we honor their time.

Like you, perhaps, I found myself defining my sense of worth and value based on the success of my business. It fueled my ego and fed my belief that

I was paying off bills and creating an economic future of choice for my family. That of course included a beautiful home, nice vacations, paying for parochial school tuition, saving heavily for college education, and planning for retirement. Does that sound familiar?

I found myself developing a practice where I was working for everyone else except me. I employed two administrative people, two Chairside assistants, two Expanded Function Dental Auxiliaries, and two hygienists. Big numbers, big production was the name of the game . . . or so I thought. After all, I was working to be the biggest, baddest, fastest, coolest, wealthiest, and most respected dentist in town. I was unaware at the time that I was learning the lesson that a manager cannot both lead the band and play all the instruments.

Clueless, I was adding to the horrific speed needed to keep the gerbil on the wheel. I was spinning faster and faster and faster because I didn't have a clear direction in my life, both professionally and personally. I hadn't really devoted the time to discover what I was really doing; what is it that I wanted; and how did I want my life to unfold in terms of the personal side.

Now imagine this: a picture-perfect Sunday afternoon, August 7, 1988. My brother, Dr. Scott; the oral surgeon, Dr. John; and I, along with more than thirty staff persons and family members, were enjoying a wonderful, hot, sunny picnic at my home. After tossing around a football for no more than three or four minutes, without any warning, I was struck with a heart attack.

The symptoms were classic. I found myself making a private differential diagnosis at first. That is, I was evaluating in my head if I was having a heart attack, gastric upset, or I had simply overexerted myself.

I noticed that my throat was full and felt as though I had eaten a really thick peanut butter sandwich . . . without the jelly! I could barely swallow. My left arm was tingling and so was my jaw. I was sweating profusely. I was getting very irritable because the pain in my chest was just as people describe: as though an elephant was standing on it. It was scary. And I intuitively knew what was happening.

After what seemed like just a few seconds of my diagnosis, I approached my brother. Although I was in agonizing pain, I was still standing upright. I put my arm around his shoulder and said these exact words: "Brother, I'm not kidding you. I'm having a heart attack right now."

By the time we all came to a consensus that this was a very serious situation, we made a foolish choice. We drove to the hospital in our van instead of calling the emergency squad. I don't recommend this. I remember vividly sitting in the front seat of our Dodge Caravan, hunched over in unbelievable pain while watching my wife drive 35 mph (the speed limit, of course) and stuck behind two old ladies out for a Sunday drive. I admonished her for driving so slowly and strongly encouraged her to pick up the pace. Just about then, the clot must have dislodged. In an instant, I sat up and felt great. It was short-lived as the clot blocked the artery again (my right coronary artery), and the pain hit me like a sledgehammer. When I walked into the emergency room and approached the receptionist, she told me to take a seat. Speaking emphatically while clutching my chest, I quickly convinced her with all my symptoms that I was actively having a heart attack.

It wasn't long after my admission that the Metro Life Flight helicopter was picking me up for my ride to the Cleveland Clinic.

First, Stop What You're Doing

Not once during the next four days in the Cleveland Clinic did I think about my practice, my bills, or my business reputation. All I thought about was how I was going to get better, get out of this hospital, get back to my family.

I've titled this chapter "First, Stop What You're Doing," because if you don't voluntarily stop, your mental or physical health will stop you, as it did me. And that's the place where you'll find yourself taking stock, as I did. A big step was deciding that no longer would I try to please everyone. Someone once told me that if I wanted to lead a symphony, (my new life), I would have to turn my back to the crowd. I'd been taking on the impossible. No wonder it had almost killed me. So much of my behavior was driven by outside influences. I was too concerned about what others thought. The wrong motivators drove me. This "wake-up call" was what I needed to get off the gerbil wheel, or my days were to be numbered. Gifts come in unfamiliar wrappings.

CHAPTER 2

How'd I Get Here Anyway?

WHERE DOES THE HUNGER FOR APPROVAL COME FROM? How do children grow into adults who want to overachieve or please at all costs? How does "stinking thinking" hamper us?

Emerging from a dysfunctional childhood is not my story alone, but I raise these questions so that you might examine your own journey, and the people in it—those who were encouragers and those who held you back.

My parents split when I was a preschooler, and my mother's choice for a stepfather was a bully named Tommy. By the time I reached high school, I had grown to resent Tommy because he ridiculed and criticized me constantly. I would do anything to stay away from home. To him, I was never good enough, never did anything right—and that's the way I felt. Tommy would bark, "Sit up straight. Use your fork. That's not the way to eat. You're not holding the shovel the right way. You cut the grass the wrong way." To others these comments may seem innocuous, yet when you hear them again and again and again they have a profoundly negative impact on your psyche.

When I recall those times, I now know how my low self-value was sown. After years of being told you're not good enough, you begin to believe that crap, whether it's true or not.

On the other hand, I don't know how Tommy put up with me. He made a commitment to raise me and my siblings, and he stuck to it. I admire him for that. He just didn't know how to be a father. He got stuck in a situation he did not enjoy whatsoever.

I desperately wanted his approval and did not get it. That was just not something he thought to give, at least not to me. I don't think he had it in him.

Tommy was not the only strong influence in my young life. My biological father, Max, while unknown to me during childhood, shaped me by his absence. My size was another issue. I was always short for my age and constantly got ribbed for it. The first time I saw Max as an adult was the night before my graduation from dental school at age twenty-seven (I was three years old when he left.). It was interesting to note that he was short as well.

But there were positive influences, too. In high school, I was invited to join the Epsilons, the powerhouse sports team, non-hoodlum "gang." How I got invited is still a mystery. I was just a short little guy on the wrestling team. Epsilons did all sports-related stuff, and I didn't envision myself as a successful athlete. They were the football, baseball, and basketball stars. I was a wrestler. Who in the hell pays attention to wrestlers, especially *little* Ronnie Arndt? But now I was included in the "cool group." I had a social identity. I felt like I was somebody. The importance of being "in" something is really huge, especially for a kid with a self-image problem.

The whole time I was growing up, I felt beat down. As a result, and believing failure is not permanent, I grew hell-bent on surviving, on showing other people that I could make it. As I came to understand later, all of this made me obsessed with what other people thought of me. All their criticism ravaged my self-confidence. It also made me determined to accomplish something and shock the "naysayers."

When you carry these ideas about yourself into your young adult life and onward into a career and family, it's obvious that some of these manifestations will show up in behaviors and actions, and how you relate to other people. People readily blame circumstances in their family histories as the sole cause of behaviors. The time that I spent visiting with a psychologist after my heart attack helped me recognize that indeed past behaviors and surrounding attitudes have an impact on our personalities. However, we always have a choice. While I could blame my dysfunctional childhood and my complicated family issues as the sole reason for my self-esteem problem, that would be an injustice. The therapy helped me recognize that my future is up to me, and that "If it is to be, then it is up to me," and I could make that choice. As a matter of fact, many of the negative incidents in my life served as great learning tools. Both the positive and the negative experiences that come up in our lives enable us to create a dichotomy around which we get to decide which we prefer and which we reject. I made a conscious choice to replace my negative self-talk with positive affirmations, thus creating the glass half-full mind-set.

After my heart attack, I consciously began to shift

in many ways: my outlook, my attitude. I chose to focus not on eliminating my type A behavior, but rather on replacing it with something different.

I found myself feeling more calm, not as anxious, not worrying so much. I did not have to be in such a hurry. And it began to show up in the way I connected with my kids and my family.

I affirmed my new life direction by codifying my values in writing. When the kids wanted or needed more attention or a special time with Dad to simply "play," I played. I made a point to thank and acknowledge my wife for all she did for our family, particularly the little things like our scheduled family nights, or her little love notes in our lunch bags. Our vacations became more family focused, and I stopped taking work with me on all of our trips. By initiating a daily regimen of three-mile power walks, followed by ten to twenty minutes of meditation, I was developing a different mind-set and becoming more patient with life's typical annoyances that had formerly consumed my day. I hugged the kids more and relished the time I had with Trish, even if it was nothing more than the two of us quietly reading the newspaper together in the family room. My life was palpably changing, and for the better.

CHAPTER 3

Life Does Not Happen in a Vacuum

HAVE YOU EVER HAD A SITUATION COME up where you found yourself looking around, stunned, and asking: *What just happened? Where did that come from? How did I get here? Why am I thinking or behaving this way?* The answer lies in a complicated fact: the relationships and connections we make with people over our lifetime, when molded together, help us become who we are. What's intriguing is, many of these relationships, or connections or contacts arrive at times we least expect it. The relationship may be lifelong, or it may be measured in moments.

One that stands out for me arrived on the day I was having a heart attack. The helicopter had landed on the roof of the Cleveland Clinic. A male nurse was waiting to take me to the emergency room. He had blond hair, a full, blond beard and mustache, and the most engaging, warm, and calming smile. As I was rolled out of the helicopter, he grabbed my gurney and wheeled me through the huge doors leading inside from the rooftop. Then he looked at me and said, "Dr. Arndt, I am not going to let you die." He was like an angel. I never got his name, and I never saw him again. But I'll never forget him. At that moment for someone to say, "I'm not going to let you die" was powerful. This man's life touched me for no more than ten minutes and yet it has had an impact on me for more than two decades.

We have all had fleeting contacts like this in our lives, as well as deeper relationships with people we've known for years. Think back over your life. Who has had a significant impact in some form that's left an indelible mark on you? Did you take away good things from that relationship? How have you applied those to your life?

As a teenager, I was lucky to have a surrogate father and mentor in Mr. Mike Melnyk, the father of a girl I dated for a short period of time in high school. I was brokenhearted when the romance

Life Does Not Happen in a Vacuum

between Nancy and me didn't bloom, but even after we broke up, I kept inviting myself to her house because I had developed an incredibly warm and close relationship with her parents. I'd say "hi" to Nancy and immediately go to the kitchen and visit with her parents for hours and hours. In fact, I spent more time with the Melnyks than I did with my own family.

Mr. Melnyk was short, like me. He had a slight balding hairline and an incredible smile that said, "C'mon Ronnie, let's talk." He could make me feel special and valued. Mother Melnyk was always nearby, giving words of encouragement, helping me select my latest girlfriend, always reminding me of the importance of my college education and to not let anything get in the way. She could be stern, but under this toughness was a warm and insightful woman.

Through the years, every Easter, every Christmas, and every weekend home from college, that's where I went first. I never wanted to go home. I would sit and talk with the Melnyks about everything and feel so whole, so special, so loved. They became the parents I had desperately needed. And they symbolically adopted me as the son they never had. As my life unfolded, Mr. Melnyk unknowingly became my "northern direction."

I am alive today thanks to the unqualified love and attention they gave to me when I so desperately needed parents. So, while I didn't get Nancy, I got a set of parents in this special couple, who gave me the critical tools I needed to fashion a life.

The Melnyks became a precious part of my life. They were at my college graduation, dental school graduation, and my wedding. Years later, at my daughter Brianne's baptism, I noticed that Mr. Melnyk looked really tired and his movements were slower. I knew something wasn't right. I don't know what came over me, but I walked out to where he was standing several hundred yards on the opposite side of our pond. As usual, he was smoking. I walked up and took the cigarette out of his mouth, threw it on the ground, wrapped my arms around him, and told him that I loved him. We hugged for what seemed like a few minutes. He, like me, was a bit astonished as we had never said these words to each other, nor had we really hugged like that.

This was my single most important life lesson: do not wait to tell someone you love them, care for them, and tell them that they are special to you. Tell

Life Does Not Happen in a Vacuum

them *today*, for tomorrow may never come. This lesson, above all others, has changed my life. Shortly thereafter, Mr. Melnyk died. Naturally, I was devastated and yet so pleased that he knew how much I loved him.

It's funny how life magically unfolds. I dated Nancy a few times, met her parents, and they became two of the most important people in my life.

Who are the important people in your life?

What needs to be said to them before it's too late?

How can you let them know how much you appreciate them?

CHAPTER 4

Gerbil Wheel Dynamics— He Can't Run Forever

I MISTAKENLY THOUGHT THAT MY SUCCESS, both business and personal, was tied to an unfounded belief—that my worth was solely based on how successful my dental practice was. After all, I had to impress my peers, I had to impress my spouse, and I had to impress my then-new friends with the idea that I was some successful young dentist. Little did I know the negative energy I was accumulating would have an effect on my health and all my life relationships.

I was either too arrogant and thought I knew it all, or I was just too damn stupid to step back and think about this gerbil lifestyle and what it was costing me.

The success of my practice defined who I was, my personal self-worth, as well as my external view of myself. Although I denied it at the time, there were times when it became clear to my wife that my practice was the most important thing in my life . . . and not her. That was one of my major life mistakes.

Now, as a more mature man, it's easy to understand the brashness of youth. I continued to push and push and push. I worked harder. I expanded my hours thinking that I needed to appeal to the marketplace and patients that needed to be seen after work in the evenings, on weekends. You name it, I'd be there. Foolish thinking, as it was unknowingly taking a toll on me. I expanded my staff thinking that more, and more, and more production was the key to my success. I never gave a thought to life balance. I continued to add more expense to an ever-increasing overhead without knowing it because in my never-ending drive to succeed I had failed to track my practice numbers with any regularity. I had not given much thought to disability overhead coverage or the value of developing a financial savings strategy to protect my family and my practice investment.

After my heart attack, I knew I had to make some major readjustments in my life. Otherwise, I'd be back in the same situation, and maybe even worse. Because what I did learn is, the most common first sign of heart disease is sudden death.

While I was recuperating in the hospital, I had an epiphany. All of a sudden, I knew *why* I'd had a heart attack. It wasn't my bad habits. It wasn't my family history. It was my "stinking thinking." Unbeknownst to those around me, in my mind, my glass was always half empty, and I carried that feeling around with me everywhere I went. It resided in my self-talk, the quiet, unobvious, and negative communications I was having with myself. For my entire life I had masterfully disguised my feelings of "less than" with an outer façade of strength and "I can do it." It was finally exposed to me. I finally came face-to-face with my internal truth!

At the end of my first day at the hospital, I fervently asked the cardiologist to bring me a psychiatrist. He looked down at me through his reading glasses perched on the end of his nose, and said: "I'm the doctor here, and I make the treatment decisions."

The next day I asked him again, "I need to see a psychiatrist. I know why I had a heart attack. It's my 'stinking thinking,' and I need to talk to someone who can help me. I need the help desperately." He looked at his chart, offered another snide "I'm the doctor" comment, made a notation in my patient chart, and quickly exited the room.

Later that day, a woman quietly and majestically walked into my room. She was wearing sandals and a long skirt under her white coat—a real hippie-type doctor—and she introduced herself. She talked with me for nearly thirty minutes, a short time really, but it was life changing. I don't remember what she said, I don't remember what I said, but something *huge* shifted for me. In retrospect, I understand that the more words you use, the greater the chance of being misunderstood. This doctor's words were few, laserlike, and healing.

I had a new attitude. Never before had I opened up to someone so completely and in such a short period about whatever history had prevented "me" from being "me." She masterfully guided me with her questions and insights to help me discover that I was now beginning the first day of a "new life."

Before then, I always, *always* compared myself to other people, struggling to be better than the other person. I had to be successful. I had to be the best. I could be impatient and demanding, because

I was single-minded in my quest to get ahead as quickly as possible.

Back then, I was striving to be successful according to how other people defined success. I wasn't striving to be happy on my own terms. I suppose I was trying to prove something, perhaps the result of pent-up emotions from my childhood.

What I want for you, the reader, is to *not* wait for a major health issue, or a failed relationship, or any other kind of trauma, to encourage you to make some shifts in your thinking that could potentially save your life. You don't have to be like me, you don't have to ignore all the signs and symptoms, and wait for a near tragedy to strike. If anything that I have shared thus far resonates with you, you know that it is important to get off that gerbil wheel. However, to do that, you must be willing and resolved to take action. You must have a desire for something different. You must want to vote for your life.

Everything in life is about give and take. You never take anything without giving something in return. Success in life becomes more of a reality when you're clear about your expectations. Unclear expectations lead to unclear outcomes. And nothing we do in our life, nothing, is immune from consequences. While oftentimes we may feel that those consequences are unfair, unintended, or inappropriate, be prepared for them. When we are young we somehow feel that we are immune or have a superhuman resilience to the laws of life. Not so—"life" offered up its consequences for me.

While I didn't say it was easy, the solution is rather simple: jump off the wheel. Over the following pages, I'll share with you some ideas that have worked for me and may work for you. What's beautiful about this process is that you get to decide the degree of change that you want for yourself. In my case, I chose massive and fast change. For you, it may be grabbing the low-hanging fruit and moving forward in a slow and methodical pace. It's your choice.

CHAPTER 5

What's Most Important?

AFTER TALKING TO THE PSYCHIATRIST IN the Cleveland Clinic, I knew that I needed to take a real honest look at my belief systems, as well as how I felt about myself, and rewrite my self-talk. I needed to leave my comfort zone. I knew I had some unhealthy behaviors that had accumulated over time and had resulted in my heart attack. Most people would think it was physical, but I believe it was personal, emotional, and mental. I now knew that I needed to get a far better handle on what was important in my life, how to create balance, and how to prioritize the things that were really important to me. As Larry Winget reminds readers in his book *Shut Up, Stop Whining & Get a Life*, no one was going to give me what I wanted. It was up to me. This was a huge tipping point in my life.

Over that five-week recuperation period, I began what I describe as the metamorphosis of the new Ron. I worked hard to repaint my portrait with self-worth. I thought about work, but I admit that I spent very little time thinking as intently about my practice, because I knew that the focus had to be on me. I knew that I needed to get healthy, so I could be helpful to others.

The five weeks away from the practice gave me a wonderful opportunity to reconnect with my family. Trish and I did many things with the kids that were so simple, like sitting and talking with them. We laughed a lot. We had a one-acre pond, so I swam and did the kinds of kids activities and games that they wanted to play, healthy things between a father and his children. I was also able to recommit my love to Trish, and remind her just how important she was to me, now and always.

I was able to chill out. I became interested, involved, and excited to learn about meditation. This became a passion—learning how to meditate. I thank God for Dr. Shad Helmstetter's books, *What To Say When You Talk to Your Self* and *The Self-Talk Solution*. I devoured them, marked them up, wrote in them, and applied his ideas with explicit detail. These two books were instrumental in saving my life.

I was reading many, many books—most of which were about self-improvement. Nathaniel Brandon's books on self-esteem were extremely valuable in enabling me to shift my thinking. I also spent two solid weeks every day visiting a young, energetic psychologist to focus on developing a much healthier mental outlook on my life. I knew that by shifting my thinking, by developing alternative belief systems, I was going to come back from this heart attack with a much fresher outlook on life, and a clearer perspective on what I wanted, and where I wanted to go. No excuses. No blaming. No more drama. Just 100 percent commitment.

To create this direction, I knew I had to identify my core values, the guiding principles around which I would make all of my business decisions. They would serve as the litmus test against which I identified what was "right" and "honest" for me.

I knew that these core values would be the genesis of everything that I wanted to do in the transformation of my practice. I set aside several thirty- to forty-five-minute quiet-time periods, so I could work on identifying my core values. As a basis for this process, I used the following elements:

1. My core values are ideas that I want to publicly affirm;
2. My core values are ideas that I greatly prize and have a positive influence on my life;
3. My core values are ideas that I am willing to act on;
4. My core values are ideas that I would repeat if given the circumstances again and again; and,
5. My core values are ideas that I choose freely and with a clear understanding and recognition of the consequences of my choice.

I made notes, and I revisited them from time to time, until I had identified those governing values that clearly identified who I was, both as a person and ultimately as a dental practitioner.

At that point, I codified my core values. I put them in writing.

By first identifying my personal core values, I was then prepared to develop and present my business core values publicly, first to my team, then to my patients. My personal values served as the foundation to the incredible process I will be sharing on the redesign of my business model. Again, yours probably will differ, but here are my personal core values, what I call my "Thirteen Commandments":

1. **Love Yourself (A lot, without being obnoxiously obvious)**—In the same way the flight attendant demonstrates the importance of putting your oxygen mask on first, so you can then help those sitting around you. *(Love myself)*
2. **Thank Your God (Without hesitation)**—When you practice daily thankfulness, you recharge your soul and bring joy to your heart. *(Thankful to God)*
3. **Family Trumps a Career (Life is a card game)**—What you think about most of the time becomes your reality. Thinking family regularly creates a "full house." *(Family person)*
4. **Touch Your Spouse (Do this a lot, too, without being obnoxious)**—Give a little piece of yourself every day to the person you love the most. It doesn't cost a cent . . . and the return is immeasurable. *(Great husband)*
5. **Nourish Your Legacy (See yourself generations out)**—Our children become what we

encourage, nurture, and reward. Ultimately our children and their children become what we care about. There is no right or wrong, only consequences. *(Great father)*

6. **Honor Your Handshake**—Your life becomes a reflection of how you ultimately treat others. *(Honest)*

7. **Set Examples Daily**—Low morale, bad attitudes, and insolvency are unflattering to a leader. However, high expectations and clear vision, followed by consequences, are not. *(A leader)*

8. **Regard Yourself Well**—What happens when you get knocked down? Do you pick yourself up, brush yourself off, and move forward? It's not what happens to a man; rather, it's what he does with what's happened to him. *(Respected)*

9. **Wealth Is Not Only What You Have But It Is Also What You Become** —By serving others, success and money almost naturally appear. *(Financially secure)*

10. **Use Your Smarts**—Where you talk less and listen more, the smarter you appear to others and the more you are recognized for being a marvelous conversationalist. *(Intelligent)*

11. **WII-FM (The worldwide radio station)**—

When you look for the good in other people, and you tell them what you see, you become extraordinary. *(People person)*
12. **Touch-Hold-Hug**—When you take the time to share who you really are with others, you connect in indescribable ways. *(Sensitive and warm)*
13. **Think Like a Kid**—You can make life easy when you accept that failure is part of the game we play. *(Progressive)*

While these identify my Thirteen Commandments, my personal core values, yours can be very different. The number is up to you. You decide which principles would drive you to view what you know as right and true.

Here is an easy way to get started. Why not carve out some time over the next week and begin this process for yourself, if you have not already? This process will prepare you to write a compelling vision for your practice or business and for your personal life. A description of your future! What do you want your personal life to look like? How will that ultimately impact your vision for your business?

CHAPTER 6

The Workplace Makeover

WHILE I WAS RECUPERATING AT HOME, I stayed in touch with my brother and dental associate, Dr. Scott, who was holding down the fort at the office. I slowly began to psych myself up to come back to the office. Because of the way I had structured my practice and the relationship I had with my associates, I felt secure and comfortable knowing that I had another doctor making certain that the practice continued. Our patients were well cared for, and Scott was a godsend.

Thankfully, my income didn't skip a beat during my time away. As it happens, in the month before my heart attack, I had prepared a lot of crown and bridge, and Scott seated it while I was recovering. God works in unique and mysterious ways. It was one of my best months in practice and I wasn't even there. This is living proof that the definition of luck is when preparation meets with opportunity.

When I finally came back to work, I felt a heightened sense of trepidation. I was anxious, nervous, a bit foreign in my own office, because I had become so comfortable and felt so secure being at home with my family. It was in the summertime, and Trish, who was a kindergarten teacher, and the kids were not back to school, and I'd really been enjoying quality time with them. With my newly defined personal values, I did not want to leave them. So coming back into my dental practice was a bit scary.

Thoughts were running through my head, like, *Will I remember which end of the mirror to hold?* and *Will my patients accept me?* and *Am I somehow flawed?* Surprisingly to me, these warped thoughts passed through my mind: *Do I have what it takes? Can I get back up to speed?* Despite my doubts, I obligated myself to believe that anything reliably put into motion had already occurred. I set the stage for my success by faking it until I made it.

Because I was working on my self-esteem, and because I was nurturing a much better view of myself, I was able to handle reentry. However, I was not prepared for what came at me that day from certain members of my team.

I remember the morning huddle—it was fine. Everyone was attentive and affable, glad to have me back, all smiles. I explained to the team that I wanted my next couple of weeks to be low-key, not an ultra-heavy schedule. I explained what I wanted them to share with our patients, and more importantly, to make my transition back to the practice fun and easy, and then let's just get on with our lives.

And I also told the group that any staff-related issues, anything related to the business, I'd like to keep under the radar. I knew I didn't have the stamina yet, at least the mental stamina, to deal with those things immediately. I wanted to give myself a couple of weeks to ramp back up. They understood that we were going to start slowly for the first week, and then intelligently increase the pace. I explained with great clarity that I was not ready for staff or administrative hassles.

Near the middle of the day, I walked into the private office that I shared with my brother, the orthodontist, and the oral surgeon, to see two notes laid prominently in the middle of my desk. Mind you, this was my very first day back after surviving a heart attack and being out of the office for five weeks. One note said, "Are we going to get our uniform allowance today?" and the other said, "When do we get our bonus checks?"

I could not believe what I was reading. It simply said to me that in the grand scheme of things, Dr. Arndt, you don't make a damned bit of difference. We care about us and us alone. Here they were asking me for money, bonuses, uniform allowances, when they knew damn well that I'd been out of the office for weeks, and I'd asked them to go easy on me—my blood pressure was off the chart. I was outraged. Instantaneously I had reverted to my type A personality, and I was horrified to realize all my five weeks of work had disappeared in an instant. When my brother observed how upset I was, I think he was probably afraid that I might "heart attack out" on him again.

Scott had to calm me down, physically and emotionally. I could not walk out into the office floor—into my treatment rooms—for at least ten minutes. I managed to get through the day—I don't know how. Later, as I was wrapping up and no one else was around, the two of us were sitting in our office. Soon I'd be leaving for home and I'd have to explain this to my wife and my family. I had heard the phrase, "Accept that some days you're the pigeon, and some days you're the statue." That day I definitely felt like a filthy, disappointed, and angry statue.

I said to Scott, "I want you to know that within three months, I am coming back to you and this team with a completely different practice. I will never let this kind of stuff happen to me again. No longer will I allow my practice to dictate my professional and personal life in such a way that I lose control of having it the way I wanted it."

I was true to my word. I had already established my Thirteen Commandments, my personal core values. They were the foundation on which I built my business core values.

For the next three months, I diligently and relentlessly began to dissect my practice, working after hours and on the weekends. This responsibility was mine and mine alone. Most importantly, I clarified my business core values, those governing principles around which I was going to make all of my decisions, the litmus test against which I would judge what I felt what was right and what was wrong and appropriate for me and my practice. I declared that in the future, I would defer all decisions to my core values—in terms of how I worked with patients, how I worked with my team, and what I expected of my team. Here's how those looked in writing:

1. **Honesty and integrity in all that we do** (Our reputation is our greatest asset)
2. **Positive and joyful** (Happiness is contagious—be a carrier)
3. **Family before career** (Above all things, family is first—including our dental family)
4. **Create raving fans** (By aiming for service to others, success and money naturally appear)
5. **Accountability** (Things that get ranked, counted, and measured get done)
6. **Listen** (We were born with two ears and one mouth—listen twice as much as we talk)
7. **Fun** (Laughter is the greatest antidote to stress)
8. **Learn and grow** (We cannot learn less)
9. **Teamwork** (It's amazing how much gets done when no one struggles to take the credit)
10. **Day is over when the work is done** (Are you interested in a professional career of service or looking for a job watching the clock from 9 to 5?)
11. **Best Always** (Your success depends on many things—but mostly on you)

While these represent my Eleven Commandments, my business core values, yours can be very different. Just as with your personal core values, the number is up to you. You decide what principles would drive you to view what you know is right and true for you in your business. Why not carve out some time over the next week and begin this process for yourself, if you have not already? This process will set the stage for you to then be prepared to write a compelling vision for your practice.

Additionally, I wrote a vision statement that helped fashion the map of where I wanted to take my practice. And through that process, I became blissfully clear about what I wanted for my practice life. It dovetailed nicely into what I wanted in my personal life . . . and that was certainly more time, and more connection with my family.

I want to encourage you to create a document that will capture your imagination. With this kind of inspiration, your employees will devote themselves to transforming your compelling vision into a reality. It will enable your team members to feel that the end results are worthwhile; it will give them a sense of direction; and it will provide criteria, so that your team will know exactly what is important or irrelevant as directed by the CEO—you!

Here's an example of what a practice vision might look like:

• • •

We lead a progressive, patient-centered, fun-loving dental practice, supported by energetic, positive, and self-motivated team members. Our practice grows through appreciative, satisfied, referring patients in a modern facility. Our outrageous patient service is effortless.

Every day is a joy.

• • •

My business core values and vision gelled during a ninety-day period, and without the knowledge of my staff, I analyzed every system in the practice—our brand, the accounts receivables, our financial arrangements, the way the phone was answered, our hours, the mix of services, the "ideal patient" that I wanted to treat, as well as the procedures I would eliminate. I clarified expectations and rewrote position descriptions; crafted our new marketing plan; wrote scripts for specific situations along with training routines; and developed an entirely new compensation plan. I literally took that practice apart, while building everything around my personal and business core values and vision.

When my plan was complete, I arranged a dinner meeting with my brother, Dr. Scott, and I explained in detail my newly designed dental practice model, where I was going, and articulated all the new elements to my practice. I wanted him to be on the same page, to understand exactly where I was taking the practice. Certainly, I wanted to know his level of interest for participating at this higher level. I won his support. Next step to come: notifying the staff.

CHAPTER 7

Killing the Practice

MY PLAN WAS TO INFORM THE STAFF OF A special half-day team meeting, a mandatory meeting, and I scheduled it for a Sunday. That's all I really told them, other than to explain that I wanted to share some important issues regarding the operation of my practice. The Sunday meeting time certainly got their attention.

When the day arrived, I was exceptionally well prepared and gleefully confident. I began by letting them know how disappointed and angry I felt on my first day back after my heart attack, and that that day was truly the genesis of this transition that I was about to lay out. I told them they could expect to hear some things that would be a shock, and that they may or may not like them, but they were free to make whatever choices they felt necessary. I had no intention of forcing any decisions, and I was quick to remind them that the scar of the unchosen surgery heals slowly. The choice was theirs to make, and I was prepared to support team members' decisions.

Going into the meeting, I was prepared for every single person to quit. I knew, above all things, I could still run that practice on my own if need be, because I *was* the practice. If you feel this approach was harsh and abrupt, consider the following: I felt the harsh and abrupt actions and behaviors by my team dictated brash, firm, and decisive actions on my part. Read on before you want to poke me in the eye.

We placed the chairs in a big circle, and I began by taking a box of tissues and throwing it to the floor. I let it sit there for a short time. I then threw myself to the floor and pretended to weep, while crying out, "The practice is dead! The practice is dead! I killed the practice! Ronald F. Arndt, DDS, Inc., no longer exists! The practice is dead!" It was quite a sight, and inside I was relieved at knowing this old practice model had come to an end!

As you can imagine, some thought I was on drugs, some thought I was crazy, but none of them really comprehended what I was doing, because they just couldn't figure out why this grown man would throw himself to the floor and cry (albeit fake tears) in front of everybody! Little did they know, they were about to learn that low morale and weak direction is unbecoming in a leader; however, high expectations are not.

After my weeping performance, I stood in front of the group and shared my revelation in plain words: "My dental practice, as you and I have known it, is dead. It no longer exists. I really *have* killed the practice. And as such, each one of you, at this very moment, is unemployed . . . you do not have jobs!"

The look of shock was apparent as team members glanced at each other looking for an explanation of "why." Some sat on the edge of their chairs, while one stood up and covered her face in astonishment. I continued: "I am inviting you to stay and share the next couple hours with me, while I explain to you what my new firm will look like. It's your choice, because I am creating a brand-new practice. Not 'just' a new practice; rather, I'm creating a new practice driven by a clear set of core values, a clear written vision, and my expectations—not my hopes or wishes—my specific and measurable *expectations*. Either you will buy in, own and embrace my core values and vision, or I will help you be successful somewhere else. Your choice! And if it's your choice, you can leave immediately!"

As you can imagine, they looked at me in total dismay.

I explained further, "When I'm finished delineating the boundaries of my new dental practice, I will excuse myself, and each of you will have the opportunity to discuss this new practice with each other. You will have the opportunity to think about it. Then you are invited, if you choose, to come downstairs and meet with me privately. At that point, you can then sit with me and interview for an open position. Remember, as of this moment, you are unemployed."

I spent the next several hours detailing exactly how I was going to run the practice. I introduced them to my core values, explained what they meant, dissecting every word and sentence. I gave them the opportunity to ask questions. I did the same for my vision, clearly laying out for them where I wanted to take the practice, again reminding them that they didn't have to own these, they didn't have to buy into any of what I was explaining. But if they didn't, they no longer had the opportunity to work with me or in this office.

For the first time ever, I became the real leader in my practice, a role that I should have assumed long ago. It had taken me years to realize that the ultimate responsibility of a leader was to facilitate their development as well as my own.

The hours were about to change, for one. "I want to come in and work hard, then leave so I can play hard," I said. That meant that in forty-five days, I was switching to a four-day, seven-hours-per-day workweek: Monday and Wednesday would be 8:00 A.M. to 3:00 P.M., and Tuesday and Thursday, 7:00 A.M. to 2:00 P.M. with a morning huddle twenty minutes prior to our first patient.

No longer would there be scheduled lunch hours. I said, "You want to have lunch, you take your lunch. We aren't scheduling breaks; we aren't scheduling lunch hours." Yes, I recognized and honored all the labor laws. I saw the advantage of the ability to expand early morning hours for our patients, and that for four days a week, we would be available to them during lunch hours. More importantly, it fit my biological clock, as I was much sharper in the morning and early afternoon. Additionally, because my brother and I flip-flopped hours and we overlapped one to two hours per day, we dramatically expanded our patient care and availability, while creating a more efficient schedule for ourselves.

As you could imagine, I heard things like, "Well, we already have our patients scheduled."

My response: "That's fine, however, in forty-five days we're going to change the schedule, and our new hours will be in effect."

I heard, "Well, I have child-care issues."

My response: "I'm giving you forty-five days to figure that one out."

I heard, "Well that's not fair."

My response: "That's interesting: life isn't fair. I am not here to be the fairness cop. I am here to tell you this is the way I am choosing *my* life, and establishing *my* time with my patients, and the balance in life with my family."

I continued to describe the mix of services that I was going to offer, one of which was, I will never, ever touch a complete denture or treat a complete denture patient, and the same is true with removable partial dentures, as well as repairing removable partial dentures. I had learned in my MBA program the power of focusing on strengths and managing around weaknesses. This area of dentistry was not a strength, was not fun, and I wasn't serving my patients in the best way possible. It was a simple decision to eliminate this phase of dentistry from my service mix.

I heard this: "That won't work. We have several patients already that were in process on their dentures."

My response: "That will work perfectly fine! Dr. Scott will take care of them. If I have to, I'll pay him to do those dentures. Never again, ever, will I do a complete or partial denture."

I then went on to explain my new fees. I raised them.

Their comments: "Oh my, our patients aren't going to like it."

My response: "Our patients won't even bat an eye." I had determined that no matter what our fees are, the patients will think they are a "little high." We had experimented several years prior when a team member insisted that our patients were complaining that our crown fees were high. For the next thirty days we offered the same crowns at half the fee. At the end of the monthlong trial we discovered three revealing facts: 1) we did no more of those procedures in this month than the average of prior months at our higher fees; 2) patients still felt the fee was a "little high"; and 3) no incentives were paid to staff as the income dropped and the practice couldn't afford to pay additional incentive compensation. I reminded them that I had no intention of using "low fees" as a strategy to grow the practice as that would be our death wish. Our patients were choosing us because our fees felt manageable and more importantly, because of how we treated them and made them feel while we served them. And for the few who might choose to leave, that's perfectly okay.

I finally made the decision that I was going to be paid what I was worth and I expected to connect my compensation with the value, the love, care, and extra attention I brought to my patients' dental health and life. No more of this conversation about if the insurance will or will not cover it. Or, "that's over Usual, Customary, and Reasonable." That old thinking had to go. My practice was not usual and customary; we were extraordinary. Here are my new fees, and those fees were to be effective immediately.

I declared: "We will train on our financial arrangements and how to discuss them with our patients . . . no more laissez-faire." My expectation was to offer up financial options for our patients that were written, fair, explained in advance, and easy to understand. And of course, any patient who'd been previously quoted a case fee was grandfathered in. But from tomorrow on, all new fees would be in place.

I proceeded to describe the positions that were available, and I detailed the specific and measurable expectations for each of the positions. Everyone was invited to reinterview for the position that they felt was most appropriate for them. In fairness to all, I explained clearly that the new wage offerings would be no less than what each was currently making.

They learned that there would no longer be paid sick time. Why? Because I did extensive research over the prior three years of all team members and discovered that when we worked Monday through Thursday, the highest incidence of sick time happened to be—you guessed it—Mondays. Well, how ironic. I learned that 67 percent of my staff sick times were on Monday. That way they would have Friday off, Saturday off, Sunday off, Monday off, forcing the remaining team to struggle through the day's patient care at only 75 or 80 percent of capacity, a costly deficit to the entire practice and huge stress on me. There would be no more of that. I made the clear decision that you get paid for being at your station, doing your job. If you're not here, you don't get paid. Much to my bewilderment, one staff person declared that the auto plant offered generous sick time, and I should do the same. Much to her chagrin, the work rules were going to be very different from the costly and unproductive sick-time policies offered by the auto manufacturers. (Note what has been the outcome of these kinds of unregulated policies on the auto industry today... discussion over!) Oh, and when you're calling in sick, I told them, no more leaving a message with another staff person or on the phone recorder. All team members were required to call me directly to explain their reason for not coming to work.

I eliminated the eye-care benefit. I made major adjustments to my benefits package, because it was being abused. It had become expected as an entitlement and was grossly unappreciated. And my staff costs had continued to escalate because of the generosity that I had built into my staff compensation package without any real consideration as to what it was costing me to provide staff services. I was now going to track my business expenses like a real businessman and compare them to industry averages to better enable me to make better decisions.

I also declared that I would no longer pay for their exotic trips to St. Thomas, the Bahamas, and Dallas. No more excursions.

Their response: "That's not fair!"

My response: "Neither is your ungrateful attitude and entitlement thinking. That's not fair . . . that's too bad. I'm not here to make certain that life is fair for you. What is fair is that you give me an honest day's work for an honest day's wage. My half of the deal is to treat you with respect, pay you a competitive wage, and create an environment where you can thrive and grow."

I expanded the continuing education credit because it encouraged their personal growth, enhanced their value, better served our patients, and was simply good business. I made people clearly aware that they would be well paid, but I was firm in my expectation: you have to show up, and produce results. Compensation would now be performance based.

Then I introduced my new incentive program: a Win-Win, Pay-4-Performance arrangement. Typically when the dental practice had a banner month, the team members stood in line with their hands out expecting to be paid more. And quite frankly, deservedly so, because collectively, we worked hard, and they earned additional income for their extra efforts. I was always a believer in sharing the wealth with my team, and I believe that behaviors that get recognized and rewarded get repeated. Problem was, I shared too much, too liberally and, in return, they had developed an attitude of entitlement. Under the new plan, when we'd have a good month, everybody would get more money. When we'd have an off month, the team would share in the losses through a unique formula that was very transparent for everyone on the team. No surprises, no finagling the calculations. It was team centered and fair. Finally, after years of feeling like it was a Win-Lose situation (win for the team and a loss for the doctor) on those months when income was down, expenses were up, and yet the team still maintained their same base pay. I now had an unorthodox plan that made me feel comfortable and simultaneously encouraged my team members to feel like they had something at stake as well. I wanted a system in place that had inherent consequences that we all knew in advance. There were no downside risks for anyone other than me, the dentist. It never felt right to pay out big bonus checks on strong months and then be in the red on weak months. So it was Win-Win, in the truest sense. Using a template I developed and with a calculator and pencil it was simply hand calculated by the team at the end of each month—easy to comprehend—the antithesis of entitlement—and the genesis of joy in the work place.

I heard: "That's not fair!"

My response: "Then *you* have a choice to make. I have made mine, and it is irrevocable."

I covered systems next: how I wanted the phone handled; what my protocol was around short-notice cancelled and failed appointments; what I expected in terms of collections; how I wanted to manage supplies and inventories; the internal and external appearance of the facility; the frequency of the team meetings and expected participation; as well as my expectations for our morning huddles. I also declared, no more part-time team members.

I reviewed every system, even though it took me nearly three hours to get through the whole process. After explaining what the new firm was going to look like, I observed everybody and they were exhausted, surprised, and in shock. I suspect that, even after hearing the seriousness in my voice and the detailed information, some of them thought I was joking. Some of them thought I was out of my mind. Some of them thought this was my typical angry self. They had seen me in the past when I was angry and frustrated, and they knew my temperament could be short and definitive. While I had been a "hothead" in the past, with my heart attack and this redesign of the firm, along with all my personal work, I was a different person. While firm in my conviction, I demonstrated no anger. And I could tell some of them recognized that I was compellingly serious.

Finally, having completed all of my comments, I invited questions. I was able to further clarify the areas of confusion to make certain that I had clearly articulated what I had intended, because when I left that room, they had to know exactly where I was going and why. My new plan of operation was based on my business core values, and as such each team member was going to have a choice. To make certain all in the room understood my every word and my intentions, I posed this question: *"What is your understanding of what I just described?"*

After all the questions were answered, I simply looked at the group and said, "Here's what will happen next: I am going to leave this room. I will go downstairs where I will be waiting in my private office. Each of you now has a career choice to make. Anyone who does not want to play with me in my new sandbox, by the new rules, is free to leave.

"I will have no hard feelings, however, I will help you be successful elsewhere. Those of you who are interested in staying with me in the new firm are invited to come downstairs and reapply for the positions that are available. The open positions are available at the benefit structure that I have recently explained, along with the new hours and all the other constraints that I have built into the new employment and compensation package. Please take as much time as you choose, and I'll be downstairs waiting for your response."

Unbeknownst to them, an hour earlier my wife had quietly entered the locked office and set up an impressive buffet of food and refreshments in the reception and business areas. The buffet was for the people who chose to stay with us. Those who chose to remain on this team with the new structure, the new fees, the updated philosophy, and the new everything. The purpose and intent was that, as a cohesive team, we were going to celebrate our new beginning. Trish and I were going to recognize them for making a personal and professional commitment to being a part of our "refreshed" team. I returned to my private office after helping Trish set up the rest of the food.

It must have been thirty to forty-five minutes before anyone came downstairs from the team development room. The time passed very quickly and I vividly remember not having one ounce of angst. My head was clear. I was so committed to this plan of action, I was so firm in my values and vision that I was unwaveringly prepared for every single staff person to walk out.

While I had no idea who would stay and who would go, I knew that I could begin the process of maintaining and growing my practice all by myself from scratch. It was freeing! There was no question that I was a man on a mission and my direction was unambiguous. Some would say I was crazy, some would say I had big cojones, but no one would ever deny I knew exactly what I wanted for the remainder

Killing the Practice

of my professional career. I discovered how freeing a vision could be.

As I had expected, one of the seven staff members decided to not apply for the vacant positions in my new dental firm. She turned in her keys, picked up her personal effects, and left the premises, never to be heard from again. That was a choice she freely made and consequently that was her last day of employment with me. Another employee was on the fence. During the interview process, I listened to her trepidation and gave her another twenty-four hours to make a final decision. Ultimately she decided to move on as well. The remaining five interviewed for the positions that were available. I assured them that their new wages would not go lower than their current level in the old firm, however all future increases in their income would come as a result of how well the practice fared. All five were rehired.

All those who interviewed and left with positions understood these were the new rules of the game. While there was some major relief among those of us who sat together that afternoon, it was still tense. We continued the discussion about my vision for the new firm in a more lighthearted fashion, as I was able to celebrate this successful "purging" around a bountiful buffet of food and refreshments. The celebration clearly was a way for me to bring closure to the old firm and recognize the new direction that we were taking.

I have always believed that my team is the greatest asset that I possess in my business. I stand behind the concept of finding and retaining a patient-focused and talented staff. In addition, I have long believed that when you evaluate a financial statement, staff compensation should be listed in the asset column. Clearly, without that team, without quality people who are committed to the same vision and the same set of values, the leader as the dental CEO is hamstrung. The doctor will be unable to create the direction of choice and the practice of choice. I was actively cheering for the success of my new team.

Time would prove that the direction that I had articulated for the practice three months after coming back from my heart attack, the ideas that I had meticulously incorporated into a new plan, and the core values and vision that I established for my practice, were absolutely perfect for me. My last four and a half years in practice were my most profitable and the remaining team members experienced the highest earning years they experienced up to this time. After all, this was about saving my life. This was about establishing a new personal and professional life and defining a balance between both. This was an exercise of putting on paper my wants and implementing in reality what was important for me.

By taking these brazen steps I could now take better care of the people I was blessed to serve. And that included my family, my patients, and my team members.

Had I not killed my practice, it would have killed me. Finally, I was off the gerbil wheel!

CHAPTER 8

The Business of Business

WHEN I FIRST STARTED AS A YOUNG dentist, freshly minted from the Ohio State College of Dentistry, I began my practice in what could be described as nothing short of a dump. I really didn't know how to find a location other than to use some common sense and evaluate demographics and community growth, and hearsay from other people. I'd visited a handful of the local businesses as well as a couple of the local pubs and simply asked questions about the community. While this seemed foolish at the time, in retrospect, it really gave me some real-life information.

I ended up working in a facility owned and operated by a family physician. It didn't take long for me to discover his medical practice philosophy and techniques were somewhat unorthodox. In addition, I discovered that after forty years of medical practice, he was as clueless about how to run a practice as I, a young dental practitioner fresh out of college.

Because I had no real business training, I had never negotiated a smart and appropriate lease. It was a terrible location, off the main drag—a pathetically ugly and unkempt building. While there was something in writing, we really did nothing more than a handshake and a couple of pages of legal jargon, and I ended up with a sloppy lease agreement. I was sharing the reception room with only spartan furniture appointments and essentially no windows. If he felt that the utility bills were getting too high, he simply turned off the air-conditioning or heat.

After a year and a half of actual practice experience under my belt, I found a much larger facility about a mile away on the main drag of town. The facility was new and attractive, however I was naïve to negotiating deals. Unfortunately I still had the privilege of paying for all the heating and lighting in the common hallways. I wish I'd had a coach then.

When I made this transition, I had enough sense to invite an orthodontist into the practice. I thought this would be a smart move—to help share the rental expense, add some camaraderie to my work, and attract more patients into the practice because I was providing specialty care. While on the surface it sounded good, little did I know of the additional stress, challenges, and obstacles that I would have to overcome bringing in another doctor whose philosophy was not necessarily parallel to mine. I also had to deal with his staff. This was simply another piece of that whole process that elevated my blood pressure.

Throughout this entire course of events, I was still making poor choices and bad hires. To be fair, I did have a couple of good employees. However, I was unmindful to how crucial the selection of quality employees would be to the success of a patient-centered practice. I had no real clue about the elements that made my practice run. Like so many dentists, especially those in denial, I thought I was so "smart" and could do it all on my own. It wasn't obvious at the time, but I certainly knew something wasn't right. I was a young gerbil and I did not notice the effects of the high speed wheel.

My heart attack changed everything. And on the day I waded back into the workflow, I realized that unless I made dramatic changes in my practice, I was going back onto the wheel. I couldn't let that happen.

Fortunately, as it turned out, overhauling my practice would save my life. I would be remiss, however, if I failed to describe that this metamorphosis was a major shock for all of us. It was one of the most challenging and pivotal moments I have ever experienced in my practice life. I'm happy to declare that the practice reincarnation was nearly seamless. Additionally, we discovered that in the ensuing months and years, the practice continued to improve and grow slowly and methodically.

I developed a great admiration for my team and the choices they made. Also, we discovered that our patients accepted our new hours with little fanfare. The team members, fewer in number and more committed to a positive future, were able to work through whatever child-care challenges they had so that within forty-five days, we actually made the transition.

Ultimately, I created a special room with couches, restroom facilities, a small kitchen; TV and VCR to enable team members to bring their kids to the office when they had "sniffles." Thus, moms didn't have to call in sick and they could check in on the kids as often as needed. This was a stroke of genius and they loved it.

I continued to remind the team that operating profitably was critically important in a business. Unlike what seems to be conventional wisdom, profit in my mind is not a dirty word. And we needed to create a profit in any way we could, as long as it was not illegal, immoral, or fattening. In *The Great Game of Business*, written by Jack Stack, I learned how to unlock the power and profitability of open-book management. Our team learned basic financial literacy.

Mr. Stack affirmed my belief that it made no sense to keep everyone in the dark about the operations of the practice. Rather, the more people knew about the business through the sharing of vital information, the more successful we would all become. This enabled us to establish goals that everyone "owned," because each of us was in a position and was knowledgeable enough about the business to do something about it and do it fast.

In my new practice, I taught my team members the basics of reading a simple financial statement. Essential to practice profitability, I felt it was very important that the team understood specific profit-and-loss line items and the impact that each one had on the practice. I coached them to track these specific line items and that the practice needed to fall within industry benchmark ranges. Surprisingly, they quickly grasped the concept of what it meant for a particular P&L number to be high or low relative to the norms in the industry. Soon the entire team was diagnostically using our financial statements to make informed choices about how to best serve our patients and operate the business profitably. It was energizing to witness dental team members making recommendations in the context of what the "numbers" told us. They learned about how they contributed to the critical numbers of the business, the benefit of writing down goals, and recognizing that you get what you give.

My team members learned that when we analyze a specific expenditure or line item in the context of a much bigger picture, we make clear and intelligent business choices. Because we were using solid accounting principles and diagnostic financial statements (designed in concert with Mr. Chris Costin, an innovative CPA) to make smart choices, I would share the numbers with my staff. I was delighted with the open-book management style.

As the leader of this dental practice, team costs, the largest cost, needed to be managed well. They all knew I expected my staff expenditures to be in a range of 23 to 27 percent of total practice receipts. Staff costs included all wages, all taxes paid by the practice, all benefits and retirement plan contributions, and they could not exceed 27 percent. I explained and educated them, using the industry benchmark research of Dr. Charles Blair, dentistry's foremost authority on practice profitability, analysis, and overhead control, that if those costs exceeded 27 percent, we had three options. First choice: increase production/collections. Second: reduce costs via cuts in staff hourly wages or eliminating employees. Or third: a combination of both.

I was resolute, and like a penny pincher.

I expected my staff costs to be at 27 percent or below. It became my mantra, as I had very vivid memories of my staff expenditures prior to my heart attack. I was determined to never operate from that old business model ever again!

My now lean and cohesive team worked diligently on our systems. We worked out financial arrangements in advance with all of our patients so there were no misunderstandings prior to treatment. We marketed the practice more from a relationship-based perspective. We connected with our patients in ways that would make them feel comfortable, valued, and appreciated. They wanted to be here with us. Pleasantly, and as planned, my team members' incomes went up, my income went up, my stress went down. We were not driven by ridiculous mass-marketing schemes requiring masses of new patients each month. We delivered simple, meat-and-potato dentistry. We were taking care of people the way people really wanted to be taken care of: the Platinum Rule blended with the Golden Rule.

I ultimately reduced my total employee count from seven to a total of three full-time employees who worked directly for me and two people that were shared between my brother and me: an Expanded Function Dental Auxiliary (EFDA); one patient-centered, full-time hygienist; another hygienist whom I shared 50-50 with my brother, Dr. Scott; plus one amazing, multitasking, full-time and a part-time administrative team that I shared 60-40 with my brother. By modifying the number on staff and working with the best possible talent, we established a climate of success. Life in my dental practice became fun and profitable while it continued to grow.

I developed and implemented a unique incentive compensation program that encouraged and fostered teamwork. When we had a month when income was down, we all, team members included, shared in the financial scarcity, and when the income increased we all shared in that as well. Compensation for my remaining team members continued to grow. Often my colleagues would ask, "How could you have worked in your practice with only one Chairside?" Simple, I hired *right*. Because Lisa, my dental Chairside and Expanded Function Auxiliary, was so exceptional, we created a "team agreement." I counted and depended on every member of my team to be "present" and attentive to our patients. Should Lisa decide not to show up for work, the administrative team knew they were to cancel out our entire day.

I had no intention of working without a Chairside and being under that kind of stress. I was a heart attack survivor, and I knew what I needed to do to make my life comfortable.

Why did this work, you might ask? By creating a series of small wins. Since everyone's compensation, doctor and team members alike, was based on the income that flowed into the business, the team knew that each and every day had an impact on their receiving an incentive at the end of the month. They did not want to lose one day of collection that could mean the difference between more money by way of bonuses in their paycheck or earning less. They now had a direct influence on how much money they could earn. I never had to motivate them . . . they did it for themselves. This was a self-managed team at its best, and it was an approach that showed people how it felt to be a winner.

The system worked fabulously well as we operated as a team. It set the stage to ensure that all my team had the same priorities, and we were focused on the same goals. Not only had I created a system that pushed them to higher levels, they pushed me as well. We had created an environment where we created greater wealth while helping the patients who entrusted their care to us. I believe in the last four and a half years of my practice, Lisa could not have missed more than two or three days because of illness or child-care issues. This accomplished lady found a way to be there by my side because the entire compensation system and the practice was built around the concept of being present, showing up, team planning, and determining your own future.

Consider these coaching questions:

1. What would you like to see differently with your team?
2. What would it take to get them "in sync" with your vision for success?
3. How would you rank each of your individual team members on a scale of 1 to 10 with "10" being high?

CHAPTER 9

My Heart Attack Gift

I'VE DISCOVERED IN MY LIFE THAT oftentimes gifts come to me wrapped in packages that may not look or even feel like gifts. It takes time for that "gift" to sink in, or for you to realize its inherent value. Perhaps this has happened to you in your life? A very small note card comes your way from a former employee from twenty-eight years ago. In it she tells you that the advice you gave her, and your insistence on contributing to an IRA when she was young, has now enabled her to be on the path to financial freedom. Or the daughter who, five months before graduating college, asks for personal time alone with you, saying: "Dad, I need your help to figure out what I want to do with my life." Gifts indeed, and yet neither were wrapped in bows or bright colors. Gifts that, when realized, are the essence of being human and serving others.

What have been some of the unusual or unexpected gifts, some of which may not have looked like gifts, that you have received in your life? For some, these kinds of gifts may seem obvious. For others, they are looking for something more tangible. I used to feel this way as well. I needed something real, something I could get my arms around, do, experience. Thankfully, I have also had the opportunity to learn about gifts that are not so obvious, but every bit as delicious and life changing, as well as those that I can use in everyday life.

Tell me if some of the following ideas resonate with you. I call them my "DDS Gifts."

- Daily Maintenance
- Dates
- Support

Daily Maintenance
My heart attack and the resulting impact on my life made me glaringly aware that I needed to take the initiative on a daily basis to maintain a better physical me. I make no claim to being a health nut,

My Heart Attack Gift

but I have come to realize that by taking care of me, I am much more energized and much healthier in a way that enables me to be more helpful to others. Creating a routine for improved health and doing it in moderation has been a foundational element to extending my life and reducing my stress.

Since 1988, I have been power walking three to four miles, six days a week. It's simple. You need nothing more than good walking shoes and to reserve forty-five minutes in your day. Another cool benefit . . . you don't have to look good, act buff, or get dressed up like you're going to "the club." I roll out of bed at 5:30 A.M., put on my sweats, a hat, and grab my iPod or Walkman.

In addition to these advantages, walking on the weekends and occasionally during the week with my wife has been as good as or better than any marriage counseling session I have attended. This gift of time with her has been a key success factor to our nearly four-decade marriage. We talk about each other's careers, our vacations, what is important to each other, sex, money, how to deal with issues with our children, upsets we might have with others or each other. You name it, it's fair game on our walks. The result is far better communication between us. Arguments are nearly nonexistent. We have a greater appreciation for one another. And we laugh a lot. Because laughter is the antidote to stress, walking and laughing has been a real gift.

I make no profession about being a guru or monklike, but when I come in from my walks, I treasure the opportunity to quietly meditate or pray. I set aside ten to thirty minutes each day during my workweek to calm my soul, visualize my day, be thankful for all I have, and ask for help. The results have been sumptuous. My day goes better, I have fewer surprises and the ones that come up, I am better able to handle. My stress is way down. I'm happier, and I feel like I can truly make a difference for others.

I like to finish my morning daily maintenance by reading a few pages or a chapter from an inspiring book, something that prepares me to put a smile in my every conversation. See my reference section for examples of books that can add years to your life.

What are you doing in your life when you become stressed, out of control, frustrated? What do you want to do? How well is your current plan working? Consider a Daily Maintenance that includes:

1. Some physical activity that fits *you* and your style. We don't all have to be Olympic athletes, simply participants.
2. Reserve quiet time for yourself. Read, meditate, pray, be still, anything that allows you to slow down your mind and allows you to be more energized and less frazzled.
3. Daily, either at the beginning of the day or at the end, pause for just a minute or two to be thankful. Nothing fancy, only an attitude of gratitude. This is one piece of the life-balance issue.

Dates

How much time do you take for yourself? What do you do to care for those closest to you? How are you at holding hands, kissing, being close, hugging, or saying *I love you* or *I appreciate you*? I was lousy at these things. I needed a heart attack to teach me. For you, I want something much better and without the learning curve. I want you to tap into your senses, free yourself from boredom, bad health, and cynicism.

I want you to Date. Not me, so let me explain.

What kind of respite do you give yourself during the course of the year? If you are like I was, and what I see with many of my clients, they may take one to two weeks' vacation and the majority of that time is either focused on work back home (even though they're on vacation) or spending half of the week trying to "chill out" if they can, and then getting the "jitters" thinking about when they have to walk back into the office. This is a killer! It damn near got me. I had to learn to first take more time away from my work so I could get some real rest (no work or work-related activities).

Second, I plan my calendar in advance and don't allow anything to invade that space.

Third, I do things I like and want to do. This time can be spent with family, friends, or sometimes alone.

We all know about the "battery recharging" stuff. What I want for you is something more: maximum-strength relaxation. Time away from your work where your spirit will say, "Ahhhhh." Rest that revives your senses. It took me some time to learn these techniques that are simple but challenging to adapt. How might they work for you? What is your willingness to attempt a few, or even just one of these techniques that you previously had never considered?

1. **Weekly date night with my wife.** Time to be with my Sweetness, the affectionate name I have given to my wife Trish, is a real gift. It was a weekly reminder of the times when we were dating. Sometimes we'd get all dressed up for a fancy dinner, another time movies and popcorn, and other times simply getting away from the hectic pace of home and work. Romance in any form seems to create an aura of mystique and remind us of this wondrous journey. Trish taught me that whatever you do, do it now, for there are only so many tomorrows. What do we need to do now? What words need to be said? What acts of kindness or forgiveness need to be taken today?

2. **Time with the kids or family.** Being in the present and playing games, whatever they are, seems to melt away my stress. Back when I made the conscious commitment to "play" with my daughters, Ashley and Brianne, and not think at all about my office, patients, and staff, I truly became playful and light. We wrestled, hugged, laughed and it melted away all my troubles. We created vacations that declared to the kids: "Hey, kids, you have our

undivided attention because our time is devoted to you."

The kids taught me that we don't remember things, we remember moments. Now, every time I get to visit with my daughters, it's a gift when they reminisce about what I had thought would be unmemorable or the most innocuous moments from their youth and our time together.

3. **Monthly date night with your kids.** You schedule the date, and they pick the venue. I started when they were young, and it culminated this year with my "favorite youngest daughter" inviting me to join her for a weeklong daughter-father date: a Smooth Jazz cruise to the Caribbean. Indescribable.

4. **Time alone.** What do you like to do? What are your hobbies? What inspires you to expand, be different, grow? This time can be an hour each day, a day or two in retreat, or at any venue that makes you feel peaceful and at rest. It can include other people, but most importantly, it needs to be away from work and life's distractions.

My Heart Attack Gift

I believe I may be the only dentist on the planet who does not golf, so I replaced it with other interests. I also know that women desperately need "time alone" from the myriad of jobs they perform during the day. Being a mom, homemaker, wife, money manager, organizer, taxi service, and all while holding down a full-time job is more than I can comprehend. They have my support and empathy. However, hold on, ladies. I hear the same pleas from my male clients. They feel they get no reprieve from the events that are filling their busy lives as well. They are wearing so many hats—visionary, office manager, HR director, maintenance person, PR specialist, financial overseer, marketing manager, supply manager, payroll clerk, team motivator—all while serving as the dental doctor.

One former client was in tears as he explained that after functioning in all these roles during his nine-hour days, when he got home at 6:00 P.M. each evening from his demanding dental practice, his wife handed him the kids and told him it was now his turn. While he loved his family, he needed some "quiet time," if only for thirty minutes. Tending to his flowers for thirty minutes each day was his solace and gave him his rest.

So, what do you need to do to break away and have this quiet time for yourself? Golf? Reading? College for an advanced degree? Audit an anthropology course? Gardening? Cooking classes? Spiritual retreat? Exercise? What works for you?

Support

As a dentist, I can make this claim: so many of us think we can do it alone and we don't need any help. The answer is, *not!* Even the Lone Ranger had Tonto. Show me a successful person—dentist, CEO, manager, entrepreneur, you name it—who did not have some kind of support from others. When I was a young dentist, I had adopted that "stinking thinking" and it got me a heart attack. If you have this style of thinking, what I want for you is to *stop it!* Ask for help. It is not a sign of weakness. On the contrary, it is a sign of incredible strength.

I would have loved to have a business mentor, an advisor, a real coach in my early professional life. Unfortunately, professional coaches didn't exist then, certainly not in the form we have today. It would have made such a difference if I'd had somebody who I could have bounced ideas off. Someone who knew dentistry, who had a keen

My Heart Attack Gift

insight on what it really took to be successful in business, who would really take the time to nurture my growth, to hold me accountable both personally and professionally, to kick me in the butt, and then to celebrate in my successes.

When my dear friend Mr. Melnyk was still alive, he'd watch me from the sidelines and remind me: "You may want to pay closer attention to your family," or "You may want to slow down," or "You may really want to take a look at your big picture, because chasing that elusive butterfly really may not be in your best interest." As much as I valued and loved this gentleman, I only halfheartedly paid attention to him. I only listened to what I wanted to listen to because after all I was the aspiring, successful, seemingly successful dental doctor. I wish I had had the wisdom to have listened to him more.

I want something different for you. I want you to shorten the learning curve by finding that special person. Fortunately, I had a second mentor, Dr. Hud Heidorf, who was also a dentist. I was older and was more conscious at the time of his words of wisdom. He believed that life did not have to be perfect to be wonderful. Intuitively, this man knew that kindness was the oil that takes the friction out of life, and he shared it with me in his actions. Dr. Hud demonstrated that every job is a self-portrait of the person who did it, and he insisted I autograph my work with excellence. This mentor, too, has passed and left a legacy by reminding me if you refuse to accept anything but the best, the best in your work, the best in your family, or the best in your friends, you very often get it. What I want for you is the best.

What has been your experience with a business coach or mentor? Do you have a coach? Are you a coach or a mentor to someone else? I made the mistake of not having one early on in my dental career, and I didn't listen to all the messages from my first mentor. I don't want you to fall into that trap or to take the arrogant approach to knowing it all.

Do You Need a Coach?
While I enjoyed my practice and the profession of dentistry, there always seemed to be a need, a yearning, for me to do more. Looking back, my heart attack was a symptom, a call that it was now time to step into a new role. It represented an opportunity, as did my second and third careers.

My current role as a dental coach has been a

culmination of skills I have acquired from my previous careers and life experiences. It took a heart attack to convince me that I did not have all the answers, and I couldn't do it all alone. I have the joyful experience each day of supporting clients in creating endless possibilities for their personal and professional lives. Every day when I get up and walk to my home office, I pinch myself and thank God for giving me the best career on the planet.

Working with a Professionally Certified Coach is not for everyone. The real question is: "What do you want?" I found out when working with a coach, you can expect to:

- Take more effective and focused actions immediately;
- Set better goals that are more exactly what *you* want;
- Stop putting up with what is dragging you down; and
- Create momentum so that it's easier to get results.

If this is not for you, stop and leave this page right now. No need to go any further. However, if you realize that having a support mechanism to accelerate your growth and reduce your learning curve can change your life, then take the following assessment. Please check the numbers that most represent your response. Rate your responses from 1 to 5 with "1" representing "less true" and "5" being "more true." A key follows to score your results.

1. When I make a commitment, you can count on it as my absolute word . . . no question.

(Less True)   1   2   3   4   5   (More True)

2. My income level has reached a plateau.

(Less True)   1   2   3   4   5   (More True)

3. *Action* is my middle name. I like taking tasks to completion.

(Less True)   1   2   3   4   5   (More True)

4. Staff "issues" are draining me of all my energy, and I'm ready to change this.

(Less True)   1   2   3   4   5   (More True)

5. I know I don't have all the answers, and I openly acknowledge I can learn a lot from working with a coach who eagerly shares his or her wisdom.

(Less True)   1   2   3   4   5   (More True)

6. In spite of my best efforts, I feel like I'm losing control of my practice overhead, and I know there has to be a better way.

(Less True)   1   2   3   4   5   (More True)

7. When I think of my business success and growth, I'm feeling frustrated, and I don't know where to begin, yet I'm looking for support and direction.

(Less True)   1   2   3   4   5   (More True)

8. Accountability, both personally and professionally, is something I could really use.

(Less True)   1   2   3   4   5   (More True)

9. I'm enormously committed to having both a fulfilling life and practice, and I'm committed to working with a coaching support system as part of my business strategy.

(Less True)   1   2   3   4   5   (More True)

10. At times I feel like I'm getting in my own way, and it's limiting my success.

(Less True) 1 2 3 4 5 *(More True)*

11. When I ask for advice and counsel from people I admire and trust, I actively apply that advice and counsel even though it might feel uncomfortable and new.

(Less True) 1 2 3 4 5 *(More True)*

12. If you were to ask my best friend to describe my personality, he/she would use words like positive, energized, committed, highly responsible, and enthusiastic.

(Less True) 1 2 3 4 5 *(More True)*

Scoring Key:

- 12-24: You're doing well . . . perhaps you can model your behaviors for others?
- 24-30: You recognize you can't do it alone. A coach would really help.
- 31-44: If you want to build your business and at the same time have a rewarding personal life, do yourself a favor: hire a coach today.
- 45-60: What are you prepared to do and by when? You better do it *soon*. When you

My Heart Attack Gift

hire a coach (pronto please), ask the coach to demand a lot from you!

To learn more about the coaching profession, you can visit the International Coach Federation (ICF) Web site at www.coachfederation.org. Formed in 1995, the ICF is the largest worldwide resource for professional coaches and includes more than sixteen thousand members who are dedicated to advancing the coaching profession by setting high professional standards, providing independent certification, and building a network of credentialed coaches.

I have chosen to participate in this organization because it exists to enhance and advance the coaching profession through programs and standards supported by members and to be an authoritative source on coaching information and research for the public.

You are also invited to visit my Web site at www.drarndt.com to learn more specifics around Dental Coaching. While you are there, be certain to subscribe to my complementary weekly electronic newsletter, *Floss Your Mind*™. In addition you will find a host of additional coaching-based resources.

CHAPTER 10

Finishing Well

I HOPE YOU HAVE ENJOYED THIS JOURNEY. While I suspect some of my ideas may not be a perfect fit for you or all your circumstances, it is my hope that there is at least one "skinny" you can pick up and apply to your life or business.

We have read so many of the clichés such as: "Life is too short," or "No one knows how much you care until you care enough," or the story of the man on his deathbed who never asks to spend one more day in the office. The unfortunate problem with these old and overused phrases . . . they are true. We are going to die. However, it is in the living that we get to create our future. Why not live our lives to the fullest and in the best service to others? How we do that is up to each one of us. I have no magical formula, only ideas to share to help you make the journey more enjoyable and rewarding.

Because I believe that "No one is as smart as all of us," I'll offer some thoughts and ideas you may want to marinade in for your own benefit.

I hope you don't have to kill your business before it kills you. If you do, I want you to know you have my support. If you don't, then congratulations, you are a lot smarter than I was. In either event, these ideas and coaching questions may just save your life:

- Just as I recognized the opportunity to hug Mr. Melnyk and tell him I loved him—why not today act on the impulse to show and tell love to those important people in your life?
- You can't learn less—what do want to learn and then apply?
- We remember moments not things—what memories do you want to cherish?
- How much is enough?
- I didn't want to die and leave my kids without their dad. What additional attention needs to be paid to your children or family members or friends?

- The Lone Ranger had Tonto; Mickey had Minnie; Abbott had Costello; Romeo had Juliet; Adam had Eve; Batman had Robin; and Peanut Butter has Jelly . . . who do you have?
- Huddle . . . a lot. They do it on the football field, and it works. They do it on the soccer field, and it works. It works in real life, too. I want to encourage you to huddle more, to hug, to talk, to share, to be close, to express love with those family and friends that mean so much to us.
- My mentors and my coach, Chrissy Carew, MCC, taught me that the most important trip you make in life is to meet people halfway. She challenged me in a big way and I pass on this challenge: *What if you went all the way?*
- Days after coming home following my heart attack, I took time to privately record my thoughts and feelings using an old audiocassette recorder. Eighteen years later, I had it transferred to a CD and gave a copy to each of my daughters as a gift, to remind them of how much I loved them. What do

you want to record and pass on? Remember, when an old man or an old woman dies, a library closes. You are a library. Why not share your brilliance and wisdom? Before it's too late!

I firmly believe that when you live from "abundance," every problem or challenge becomes an opportunity. By seizing upon these opportunities, I accumulate more in wisdom, love, passion, and money, which enables me to help others.

When I think of my future, several quotes come to mind:

> *Celebrate what you want to see more of.*
> —TOM PETERS

I plan on celebrating, taking advantage of, and cherishing the time I have with Trish and the kids. I love them unconditionally.

> *The difference between ordinary and extraordinary is that little extra.*
> —JIMMY JOHNSON

I plan on delivering that "little extra" in everything I do, in both my work and my relationships.

Our growth depends not on how many experiences we devour, but on how many we digest.
—RALPH V. SOCKMAN

While I do not know how many more careers I have left in me, whatever my work is, I want to remain passionate and alive about the outcome.

The best portion of a good person's life is the little, nameless, unremembered acts of kindness and love.
—WILLIAM WADSWORTH

I want to continue to do all I can to help others feel better about themselves through kindness and love. I love the feeling I get when I can be helpful and kind to others.

And finally:

Every job is a self-portrait of the person who did it. Autograph your work with excellence.
—ANONYMOUS

It is my intention that whatever is left in my life to do, I plan on doing it with panache.

My life has been a gift from God, and sharing this story with you, and those who reside in my heart, is also a gift. So how do we finish well? I shared with you, so now you tell me.

> *No one is as smart as all of us.*
> —Dr. Ron

RESOURCES

Web sites:

American Psychological Association: www.hardcore-stress-management.com/stress-statistics.html

Ronald F. Arndt, D.D.S., M.B.A., M.A.G.D., MCC: www.drarndt.com

Chris Costin, C.P.A.: www.costincpa.com

International Coach Federation (ICF): www.coachfederation.org

Dr. Charles Blair & Associates: www.drcharlesblair.com

Further Reading:

Beckwith, Harry. *What Clients Love: A Field Guide to Growing Your Business*. New York: Business Plus, 2003.

Blair, Charles. *Coding with Confidence The "Go-To" Dental Insurance Guide (2009/2010*

Edition) and The PracticeBooster® Clinical Treatment Intensifier^{SM} (CTI^{SM})

Blanchard, Kenneth, and Spencer Johnson. *The One Minute Manager.* New York: William Morrow, 1982.

Godin, Seth. *Purple Cow: Transform Your Business by Being Remarkable.* New York: Portfolio Hardcover, revised edition, 2009.

Gross, T. Scott. *Positively Outrageous Service: How to Astound and Delight Your Customers and Win Them for Life.* New York: Kaplan Business, 2004.

Guaspari, John. *I Know It When I See It*: *A Modern Fable about Quality.* New York: American Management Assoc., 1985.

Helmstetter, Dr. Shad. *What To Say When You Talk to Your Self.* New York: Pocket Books, 1990.

----------. *The Self-Talk Solution.* New York: Pocket Books, 1990.

Leder, Steven Z. *More Money Than God: Living a Rich Life without Losing Your Soul.* Santa Monica, Calif.: Volt Press, 2005.

Rosenbluth, Hal, and Diane McFerrin Peters. *The Customer Comes Second*: *Put Your People First and Watch 'em Kick Butt.* New York: Harper Business, 2002.

Sanborn, Mark, and John C. Maxwell. *The Fred Factor: How Passion in Your Work and Life Can Make the Difference Between Ordinary and Extraordinary.* New York: Broadway Business, 2004.

Stack, Jack, and Bo Burlingham. *The Great Game of Business—Unlocking the Power and Profitability of Open-Book Management.* New York: Doubleday Publishing, 1992.

----------. *A Stake in the Outcome: Building a Culture of Ownership for the Long-Term Success of Your Business.* New York: Broadway Business, 2003.

Willingham, Ron. *Hey I'm the Customer: Front Line Tips for Providing Superior Customer Service.* Upper Saddle River, N.J.: Prentice Hall Press, 2002.

Winget, Larry. *Shut Up, Stop Whining, & Get a Life: A Kick-Butt Approach to a Better Life.* Hoboken, N.J.: John Wiley & Sons, Inc., 2005.

Audio:

Jampolsky, Gerald, M.D., and Diane Cirincioni. *The Quiet Mind: Imagery for Peaceful Living.* Niles, Ill.: Nightingale-Conant Corp., 1989.

Waitley, Denis. *The Inner Winner: Practice Powerful Self-Affirmation with Special Music.* Niles, Ill.: Nightingale-Conant Corp., 1986.

---------. *The Psychology of Winning: Ten Qualities of a Total Winner.* Niles, Ill.: Nightingale-Conant Corp., 2005.